I0510996

More Facebook Everything

More Facebook Everything

ALSO BY SPENCER COFFMAN

A Guide To Deception
Relax And Unwind
Work Less Live More
A Healthier You!
Affiliate Marketing Expert

MORE FACEBOOK EVERYTHING

Likes,   Shares,   Comments, Friends, Followers, Sales, And More!

BY
SPENCER COFFMAN

While every precaution has been taken in the preparation of this book, the author and/or publisher assumes no responsibility for errors or omissions, or for damages resulting from the use of the information contained herein.

MORE FACEBOOK EVERYTHING

First edition. October 2016.

ISBN: 978-1-5480926-3-4 (Paperback)
ISBN: 978-1-3708983-6-7 (Digital)
ISBN: 978-1-6622127-8-9 (Audio)

Copyright © 2016 by Spencer Coffman.
Cover Design by Spencer Coffman.
All Rights Reserved.

Written by Spencer Coffman.
SpencerCoffman.com

Do you want to discover the proven secrets to get 1000's of Facebook followers to FINALLY skyrocket your earnings with your own Facebook Page?

Do you know that Facebook has over a **BILLION** users that could potentially become your customers?

You probably know the benefits of marketing with Facebook already....

Chances are you already have a Facebook page and are waiting to start making money with it...

Are you still waiting, but nothing is happening?

The reason why you are probably not making a lot of money with your Facebook Pages is -

You don't have enough targeted Facebook fans for your page!

More Facebook Everything

It is nearly impossible for you to generate traffic or get exposure for your products, websites, or business if you don't have fans to whom you can promote...

In order to make real money using a Facebook fan page, **you need fans** - and **A LOT** of them!

How can a Facebook Page with a HUGE number of targeted fans benefit YOU?

Position yourself as a **leader in your market**

Gain HUGE exposure for yourself and your business

Get **more traffic** to your websites and products

Generate **bigger profits** and make more money online

Luckily, you have stumbled across this book today, because More Facebook Everything is going to show you how you can finally drive more targeted fans to your page that will be interested in what you have to offer.

I will show that YOU can -

Get targeted Facebook fans quickly and easily to make more money with your own Facebook page.

I have created an excellent book on **how to get more targeted Facebook fans.**

After you have gone through this book, you will have no problem *getting more fans to your Facebook pages, and making money with Facebook will be A LOT easier for you.*

The best thing is - You can start implementing these techniques TODAY!

Introducing:

More Facebook Everything

You Will Learn...

*   How to harness Facebook Ads effectively for FLOODS of fans.

*   How to use Social Media and Social networking sites for more targeted fans.

*   How to use Viral Videos for huge amounts of fans.

*   External websites that you should use to skyrocket your fans and profits.

More Facebook Everything

*   How to use plugins to increase your fans tenfold quickly and easily.

*   How to use outsourcing sites to dramatically increase your fans for cheap.

*   And much more that is too secret to disclose on this page...

You can see that More Facebook Everything is the complete package you have been waiting for.

Follow the simple steps and you are almost guaranteed to increase your traffic and sales.

It's easy to see how this great book will benefit your business if you grab it today.

It time to make a decision my friend...

Do you want to continue looking for new ways to get more exposure for your business, trying to get more traffic and make bigger profits, OR do you want to **QUICKLY get MORE targeted Facebook Fans that can earn you thousands of dollars?**

The choice is yours.

"Yes! I really want to discover how to get more Facebook fans faster and get tips, hints, and secrets that will give me the edge in social marketing.

So please send me my copy of "More Facebook Everything" - so I can start getting more targeted Facebook fans and finally making bigger profits, starting today!

Claim Your Copy Today!

More Facebook Everything

More Facebook Everything

Table of Contents

Create A Product Giveaway Campaign

Create And Use Lead Magnets

Capitalize On Photo, Video, And Name Tagging

Purchase "Likes" From Freelancer Websites

Take Advantage Of Viral Videos

Create Your Own Shop Inside Facebook

Conclusion

Appendix: Resources

Introduction

If you want to increase your business through social networking then there is really only one social network site that you need to join, and that is Facebook. The reason is that Facebook has monopolized the social network market. It is a social network that nearly everyone has heard of, and billions of people use.

The fact that you are reading this book means that you are probably aware of the great marketing possibilities of this huge social site. Chances are that you have already created your own Facebook fan page, have experimented with marketing it, have joined other social networks and may have even started using, or considered using Facebook ads. It is also likely that you have done all of this without much success. After all, that is why you are reading this book.

As you very well know, the largest obstacle that you will face is getting more Facebook likes, shares, and followers. In reality, the bottom line is that it is impossible to make money on your Facebook page if you don't have people who follow and like your page. Therefore, a few of the great tactics you will learn in this book are...

More Facebook Everything

How to get targeted fans that will like your page

How to get people interested in your products or business

How to convert fans to paying customers

How to keep fans, followers, and customers for life

How to make money with your Facebook marketing

And Much More!

This book is written for people who already know how to set up a simple Facebook page or who already have a Facebook page. If you don't know how to set up a Facebook page, then check out the Social Media How To Videos by Spencer Coffman on YouTube. There, you can learn all about how to set up a Facebook page, as this book is not going to address that in full detail.

With that said, let's get on with the book so you can learn how to start getting lots of traffic to your Facebook page. Please read each section carefully so you will fully understand the content. Then, try to implement the techniques as soon as possible. That way, you will be able to get more high converting traffic to your Facebook page right away.

Best of luck!

Why Facebook?

Facebook has over one billion users every month. Therefore, it is very important for any online business to be able to establish a strong presence on this popular social networking site. Think about it, even if you promote your business and only reach a fraction of the one billion-plus active users, you will still be sitting very well. Take a look at the math for a second.

Facebook has over one billion users every month. Let's say you were somehow able to reach ten percent of those users in one month. Ten percent! That would be a whopping one hundred million people!!! How about if you only reached one percent of the active Facebook users? That would be ten million people, in only one month! In order for your page, site, product, blog, or whatever, to go viral you need to have about ten thousand views a day for at least five to seven days in a row. Ten thousand is one thousandth of a percent of one billion. Therefore, if your ad only reaches one thousandth of a percent of the active Facebook users, then you will have reached ten thousand people.

If you promote your business through Facebook and reach only a fraction of the one billion active users, there is no denying that the impact to your business will be huge. Creating a Facebook fan page is arguably the best way to promote your business through Facebook and getting lots of likes from Facebook fans is undeniably the only way for your Facebook page to be successful.

In order for your Facebook page campaign to be successful, you must be able to get lots of likes from Facebook users. A Facebook user who likes your page officially becomes your fan, which is also the equivalent to having them subscribe to your page. Once subscribed as a fan, these users can view all the updates, offers, services, and any other information coming to-and-from your page. The posts to your page will show up directly in their Facebook home feed. They will also be given a notification that there is a new post on your page.

These two features alone make informing people about your products much easier. Now, instead of sending out a mass email, or some other form of expensive communication, all you have to is post an update on your page and all of your followers will immediately be notified. In addition, anyone who likes your page can share any of the posted content to their own timeline. This makes your post visible to all of their friends. It also means that when they share your post, all of their friends will now see that post in their Facebook home feed. Are you beginning to understand the power of Facebook marketing?

You have a page with one hundred followers. You create a post and that post will show up in the home feeds of one hundred people. Then, one of those people shares your post to their timeline. Now your post will show up in all of their friend's home feeds. If they have one hundred friends, then your post is now visible in one hundred more people's home feeds. And the reality is that most people have more than one hundred friends. Therefore, take advantage of Facebook and all it has to offer. Start creating, and perfecting, your Facebook page right away!

More Facebook Everything

Creating Your Page

In the world of Internet marketing, building your presence on a popular social networking site such as Facebook is one of the most crucial decisions that you can make for your online business. Facebook has more than 1.1 billion active users that exchange trillions of objects such as web links, stories, blog posts, photographs, and videos each and every month. If you are able to build a strong web presence on Facebook through the use of a Facebook page, your business will skyrocket. Guaranteed. Think about it, 1.1 billion people on Facebook every month. Where else do you have the opportunity to expose your page to that many people in one place? Nowhere.

Learning how to leverage Facebook to increase your exposure and generate traffic to your business is essential. In fact, it is so crucial that the amount of traffic that you generate from Facebook alone could mean the difference between your failure and your success. In order to promote yourself, your business, your products, or whatever, you need to have a Facebook page.

Creating a Facebook fan page is easy. Hopefully, you already have a page created, but in case you don't, here is a very brief tutorial. Remember, that there are excellent how-to videos in the How To Social Media Playlist by Spencer Coffman on YouTube. Watch the videos and you will learn how you can set up all the social media accounts you need. There you will see how you can create a Facebook page. The following paragraph will provide you with an overview. However, if you don't have a page, then you should watch the video because it will really help you to see how it is done, rather than reading how it is done.

The first thing you need to do is log into your Facebook account. Then you will use the "create a page" link either on the sidebar of the home screen or by using the drop-down arrow in the upper right corner by your name, privacy, settings, et cetera. You can then create a personal or business fan page as long as you agree to the Facebook Terms of Use. Once you have chosen your page category, you can proceed with entering all of the details about your page.

Creating your page and entering in all of the details is the easy part. The tricky thing is how you can get people to like your page after you create it. You see, a Facebook page is useless unless you have fans. The main purpose of a page is to reach out to the Facebook users, so it is very important that you build a strong following of Facebook fans if you want to succeed. One of the ways that you can do this, and hopefully it is already done, is by making sure to fill out ALL of the details about your page.

This means that you need to have paragraphs of written information describing what your page is about. Make sure you have links, names, contact information, and anything else that Facebook suggests. This will greatly help to promote your page. Facebook will take all of those settings, details, and any other information and use it to suggest your page to other people who match your interest description. Therefore, it is essential that you have all of the information filled out. That way, Facebook will promote your page for you, for FREE.

So, if you don't already have all of the details filled out for your page, or pages, take a break from reading this book and complete that task right away. You must fill out ALL of the information to the best of your ability. Take the time and do it right. Get it filled out and Facebook will index your page and begin suggesting it to potential likers right away.

More Facebook Everything

Using Facebook Ads

Once you have your page created and have all of the details filled out, you are ready to promote your page. Where are you going to promote it? Why on Facebook of course! Remember, Facebook has a potential audience of 1.1 billion people. That is a huge market. Why would you promote your Facebook page anywhere else? You'll find out some reasons later. However, by far, the best place to promote your Facebook page is on Facebook itself.

If you are willing to shell out a little bit of money for advertising, the most effective way to achieve lots of Facebook fans quickly is through the use of Facebook ads. If you are serious about promoting your product then you will have a budget for advertising. Every good business knows that in order to make sales you need to advertise. Therefore, if you weren't planning on spending money for Facebook ads then you need to rethink your strategy. If you want to get likes to your page and start converting those likes to sales, then you need to start using Facebook ads.

Take a look at Facebook. Log in and start visiting some pages. Every time you visit a page you will see other related pages and different ads placed on the right side of the screen. There is a whole strip of them. Do you think those ads work? You bet they do! Remember, over a billion people have the potential to see those ads. Of course, Facebook is only going to promote your ad based on the parameters that you specify. This is a great thing because it means that your ads will be targeted towards people who are already interested in what you are promoting.

Think about it, if you are selling wedding products, do you want your ads to go to single unmarried men, or do you want them to go to recently engaged women? You want your ads to be targeted to an audience that is currently in the market. If you are selling baby strollers you want your ads to go to pregnant women, not to single men interested in hunting and fishing. By using Facebook ads, your ad is guaranteed to be placed in front of the best potential market for your product.

Think of all the data that people enter and post on Facebook. Facebook knows exactly what each and every user is interested in, Facebook knows your relationship status, what you do for fun, what kind of phone you use, your computer, where you live, what you like to eat, and so much more! They take all of that data and use it to profile people. They do so legally because, after all, every Facebook user is voluntarily creating their own 'Facebook Profile'. Therefore, in addition to each user-generated profile, there is also a more detailed and stereotyped profile created by Facebook.

Facebook takes your ad and matches it to the profiles of different people. This is why Facebook ads are so effective. Because people are seeing ads that they are already interested in. Facebook knows they are interested in them because the person has been profiled and fits the profile of the ad. This is so great because you can use your ads as a platform for getting likes from a lot of seemingly random Facebook users. When in reality, they were targeted and profiled to be potential buyers for your product.

See why Facebook ads are so effective? Hopefully, you do and are convinced that you need to start using Facebook ads to promote your page right away. The following paragraphs explain a little bit about how you can set up your Facebook ads.

The first thing you need to do is log in to your Facebook page and click the "Create an Ad" link which is usually located on the right side of the page. Often times, it is shown next to all of the other Facebook ads. It is very important that you are logged into your Facebook page and not your profile. You must be viewing your page as the administrator of the page. You need to be liking, sharing, commenting as the page, not your personal profile. This is extremely important. Log in and go to your page as your Facebook page. Then click the "Create an Ad" link.

After that, you will be prompted to set the parameters for your advertisement. This is the part when you specify the profile for your ad. Facebook will use your parameters and match it up with the profiles they have created of their 1.1 billion users. Then, when they find a match, they will place that ad on that person's Facebook account for them to see. This is why it is important that you set accurate and detailed parameters for your ad. In addition, you must have all of the details filled in for your page so that Facebook can use that information as well.

Some examples of the details that you will set for your ad include the target location. Do you want your ad going to people in the US or to the whole world? Or perhaps you are advertising for a local product and you only want it to be displayed in your state, or maybe only your city. You can also set the age group. For example, are you targeting teens, adults, or the elderly population? Think about who would be most interested in what you are advertising. Who is your intended audience? Find that out and you will be able to set all the parameters without any trouble at all.

A few more great details that you will want to add would be the sex of your audience. Are you marketing primarily towards men or women? In addition, how about the relationship status of the individual, is your page for single individuals, married people, or everyone? Think about who would be most likely to use whatever product you are marketing. You must think of as many factors as you can. Be specific. However, at the same time, you want to make sure you have broad enough specifications so that you are not limiting your audience.

Be sure to specify the targeted interest groups that are related to your page. For example, is your page related to online shopping, affiliate marketing, cleaning, health and fitness, et cetera. Set these parameters carefully and do so with thought. Make sure that you are inclusive and specific. You need to think like a retailer even if you are not selling a product. Because, in reality, you are selling a product. You are selling your page, or more specifically, likes to your page. You are trying to sell something to someone that they don't even have to pay for. You would think people would be lining up to like pages and support anyone they know. However, this is not the case. People are very stingy with their Facebook likes, almost as if there is a limit or something. Therefore, you need to make sure that your ads are highly targeted because the specifications you provide will determine whether or not your ads will be displayed on a specific Facebook user's screen.

For example, if you specify that your ads should only be viewable to people who are 18 and older, then Facebook users that are under 18 years old will not be able to view your ads. Your ads won't even be displayed on their screen. Similarly, if you set your ads to be targeted towards women, no men will be able to see your ad. This is why it is important that you set your parameters to target the people who will be most likely to buy your product. That way, you can make the most out of your paid advertisement.

If you are selling baby shoes and you are based in the United States, a good idea would be to set the geographical location to U.S., the age would obviously be over 18 because even though you are selling baby shoes, no baby buys their own shoes, or even has a Facebook account. In addition, you would want to set the interests to baby products and other baby related topics. Facebook will use your parameters and display your ads on the screens of people who live in the U.S., are over 18, and are interested in baby products.

When a Facebook user sees your ad on his or her screen and decides to click on it, they will automatically be directed to your Facebook page. This is an excellent way for you to get lots and lots of likes, followers, and potential customers in a short amount of time. In addition, Facebook ads are very affordable. You can choose to pay per click, PPC, or pay per impression and you can limit your daily funds to as low as $1 a day! If used wisely, creating a Facebook ad for your page cannot only bring you new fans, but it can also drive targeted traffic from users who are more likely to become paying customers. This is because they have been profiled and, essentially, hand selected by Facebook as people who will be most likely to like your page. How great is that?!

Therefore, if you haven't used Facebook ads before, or even if you have and haven't had any success, you need to start creating ads right away. Follow the steps mentioned above. Structure your ads with time, research, and thought, and you will be well on your way to achieving more likes than you would anywhere else. You will also be much more likely to have those likes convert to sales because the people who are seeing your ads are one hundred percent interested in whatever you are advertising. This is a cheat or a guaranteed result. It is the definition of preaching to the choir. Therefore, spend the time, effort, and money to start using Facebook ads for your page right away.

The Social Media Classification

There are two main types of social media sites and you are most likely familiar with both of the types. In addition, you are probably already actively engaged on several of these sites. You simply have never classified them before or never realized how they were different. The concepts for promoting on all of the social media sites are relatively the same. However, what you can do on on the different types of sites is not the same. The two main types of social media sites are social networking sites and social bookmarking sites.

The main difference between social networking sites and social bookmarking sites is the platform on which they operate. If you can build a profile and have your own little website within a network, like Facebook and Google Plus, then that is a social networking site. Other social networking sites have a similar platform. Basically, they allow you to create your own website on a general site. You have your own profile, gallery, posts, content, notes, et cetera. For a list of social networking sites take a look at SpencerCoffman.com.

Social networking sites are great for maintaining and

developing connections with people. They are network based, and many of these sites serve a purpose other than simply being social. For example, LinkedIn is a very popular social networking site that is excellent for job hunting and career building. Social networking sites can either be really good for generating traffic or really bad. The outcome depends on a number of factors that can include, but are not limited to, the topic, audience, context, purpose, et cetera.

Basically, social networking sites can be really good because people can share your posts with tons of other people in addition to reposting it themselves. This is the ultimate word of mouth advertising and that is why social networking sites can be so effective. If you post something and one of your followers shares it to his or her profile, all of their close friends and family members will probably take their word that what they shared is worth-while. The trust has already been established and, essentially, the sale has been made. You will gain fans based solely on word of mouth, which is extremely effective.

On the other hand, due to the fact that these sites can be so personal and everyone can see someone's specific activity, users may be more reluctant to share or repost information. If someone sees your post and really likes it, they may not want to like it because of the fear of what other people may think of them. They may also be hesitant because they will not want all of their friends and family to feel obligated to like the post. Remember, for some strange reason Facebook users are stingy with their likes. However, these issues are minor and should in no way scare you from promoting. If you post good content people will like and share it no matter what.

Social bookmarking sites, on the other hand, are social sites that are basically sharing only sites. They are sites where you can create a basic profile and then share and save posts to that profile. There isn't much of an option to create your own website within the site. It is basically your own personal page and that is it. Unlike social networking sites, there is no real accountability when sharing a post. It isn't published to your page or wall forever and you don't have to worry about people seeing that you like it. Social bookmarking sites are generally used with a username or screen name and are, as a result, less personal. A few of the more popular social bookmarking sites are Twitter, Reddit, Stumble Upon, and Pinterest (For a comprehensive list check out SpencerCoffman.com).

Social bookmarking sites are great for getting instant traffic because of their nature. Basically, social bookmarking sites are places where people can post and share links to websites that they like without worrying about who is going to see it or how it may be tied back to them. Some social bookmarking sites accept all kinds of links, while others are specifically focused on certain niches like news, sports, or politics. There are hundreds of social bookmarking sites out there and some of them are borderline social networking sites. However, remember, it is the platform that distinguishes them.

These sites are great because you can get a lot of extra traffic to your Facebook page or website. It also helps with your website's ranking because the more backlinks your site has, the higher it is favored by the search engines. In addition, millions of people visit these social bookmarking sites to look for the latest news, articles, blogs, et cetera, so it is a really great venue to promote your Facebook page.

Leveraging Social Media Sites

As mentioned before, Facebook ads are a great way to speed up the acquisition of page likes and followers. However, if you don't have a lot of money to spend on ads, and don't mind waiting a lot longer for your page to grow, then you can use other social media sites to help grow your page. Please note, that even if you are spending money on Facebook ads you should still use other social media sites to increase the viewership of your page.

In order for you to get the most out of social media, you need to create a profile on as many social media sites as you desire. Make sure you fill in as much of the profile information as you can. Be very detailed and descriptive. The good news is that you have probably already filled in most of this information on another website already. Therefore, all you need to do is copy and paste. However, make sure your information is written exactly as you want it and is free of errors. You want it to be as perfect as possible because if you have to go back and make a change you will have to change all of your profiles. Believe me, that can be a headache.

More Facebook Everything

Once you have filled in all of the profile information you will want to start establishing followers. Now, Facebook is your primary goal so don't be concerned with getting tons of likes, followers, subscribers, et cetera on other sites. Simply let people know you have profiles on other social media sites and allow them to connect with you. A simple way to do this is to connect all of your social media accounts and place links to your other accounts within each account. For example, on social media account A: you will place links to accounts B, C, D, et cetera. Do the same for each progressive account.

Not only is it a great idea to cross reference your social media profiles in the profile section of each account, it is also a great idea to post an update about each of your other accounts. Send a status update letting people know that they can connect with you on a different account. You will be surprised to find out that people will often click the link and add you on the other network. Remember; don't worry about gathering tons of followers on the other sites. Your main focus is Facebook. You are simply going to use these other sites as link juice and promotion to your main goal of promoting your Facebook page.

There are a couple different ways that you can leverage the use of social media websites. One is the lazy way. It is for people who only have social media accounts and are without a blog or website. It works alright, but it isn't the best. The other way requires some time and effort. However, it works very well to not only promote your page but also your blog or website.

For those of you without a blog or website, you need to get a blog or website right away. You can create one for free using Google's Blogger. Now you have no excuse to use the lazy method of leveraging social media websites. However, in case you don't want to put the time and effort into building your page properly, here is the first method of using social media sites to help drive traffic to your Facebook page.

All you have to do is simply post different links from your Facebook page to different social media websites. You can share variations of your Facebook posts to as many social media sites as you want. Then, people will see those posts and when they click the link, they will be taken directly to your Facebook page. This method is very limited because you are only sharing your Facebook page. Yes, you are sharing it in different ways, but it is all the same thing. As a result, some of the social bookmarking sites, like Reddit, for example, may shut you down because you are sharing too many links from the same URL. Other sites may not allow you to post links from another social media site. Therefore, there is always some risk in this method.

The second method is much better and it is worth the time and effort. Think about it, if you are really serious about getting likes and followers to your Facebook page, are you really going to skimp out and only post to social media sites haphazardly? I don't think so. Therefore, take the time and effort and do it right. All you have to do is create a short and simple article post. Make a very catchy title and use excellent keywords so that the search engines will index it right away. Then write a few paragraphs of content with some great keywords as well. At the end of the article, post some content about connecting with you on Facebook and then place a link that will take them directly to your Facebook page.

Make sure that you are writing about popular and trending topics. It doesn't have to be related to your business, page, or products. It can be completely random as long as it is trending. Although, depending on your business, it may be best if you write about related content. Then you need to post this short article on your blog or website. If you don't have your own blog or website, then you could also post it as a guest post on someone else's blog if they allow you to do so. In addition, you could post it on any of the online article or information databases such as Hubpages, Squidoo, Triond, et cetera (For more great sites to post articles check out SpencerCoffman. com). Posting articles to other sites is a great way to leverage social media websites without having to maintain your own blog or website. However, if you are posting on your own blog or website, then you will be better off in the long run because you will be driving traffic to your own site instead of to someone else's.

Once you have posted your article, you are ready to begin submitting it to social media websites. Go ahead and share the direct link to your article to as many sites as you want. This will get your own URL out there and drive tons of traffic to your site. These people will click on your link because it represents a

Leveraging Social Media Sites

popular trending topic. They will visit your website and read your article. Then, hopefully, they will click on the link that takes them directly to your Facebook page. You could even have a plugin-driven link, or an iframe window, that allows them to like your page from within your article. Now they will be subscribed to all of the future updates that are produced by your Facebook page.

*It may be a good idea to start posting all of your articles on your Facebook page in addition to the content that is designated as the purpose of the page. This way, the people who followed your page as a result of the article will continue to be interested because they will see other trending articles. It will also help your page seem more aesthetically pleasing because you will have posts that aren't related to your page, as well as the posts that you really want people to click on that are promoting your products.

Keep in mind, that when you write articles, you can write about anything that is popular and trending. That may include writing about things that are related to your Facebook page and the products that you are promoting. Therefore, if you are selling fishing tackle, and you write an article related to fishing in any way, shape, or form, then make sure to include some product links in there as well as a link to your Facebook page. That way you will be killing three birds with one stone when you share the link to social media sites. You will be driving traffic to your own URL, you will be promoting your product, and you will be soliciting likes to your Facebook page.

More Facebook Everything

Some more great ideas to make articles that have high readership potential are creating articles that are very informative as well as catchy. "How to" lists and "Top Ten" lists are great formats that you can use to write your articles. People love to learn how to do things and they really like it when someone has shown them the top products. People are lazy and they want their work done for them. If you have an article that shows people how to do something, tells people the top products, or compares certain products and gives them a conclusion, then you are in business.

As an example, if your business is about selling fishing tackle, then you can write an article about "the top ten biggest fish caught with certain tackle". Then post links to your products along with each of the top ten items. At the end of your article, write a convincing "hook" to get readers to want more. Something like, "click here to learn the secret to catching big fish". Then link that to your Facebook page. You can also follow that phrase with a "follow us on Facebook" link or button.

If your articles are well written, short, concise, and are about trending topics then you will have the opportunity to generate lots of traffic to both your URL and your Facebook page. Go ahead and start posting some articles and sharing them to several different social media sites right away. Remember to be aware of any rules that the sites may have (Reddit has a lot of rules).

Promote With Article Marketing

Creating a successful Facebook page with the intention of promoting your online business can be much more difficult than it seems. Often times, people get their hopes up and believe that once their page goes live they will receive hundreds of likes. Unfortunately, you will be disappointed to discover that you will be lucky to have one hundred people like your page. The reason for this is because people are not finding your Facebook page. There are millions of Facebook pages out there and unless you market your page it will get lost in the flood of pages. You need to take care to properly promote your page so that people will find it and start to follow it. Another great way to accomplish this feat is through article marketing.

Using article marketing to promote your Facebook page is so easy that even someone who isn't Internet savvy can do it. All you need to be able to do is write a good article that has valuable content. Then relate that content to your niche and conclude by linking and directing people to your Facebook page. In addition, if you can't write articles, or don't have the desire, there are a number of places that you can purchase articles to publish as your own. These are called Private Lable Rights or PLR articles. Simply purchase and publish away. Although, you may want to read through them and do a little bit of editing. Some of them can be pretty poor. In general, the best thing to do is write your own articles. That way you will be one hundred percent certain that the content is unique.

To get started you must think of a keyword, or a few keywords, that you will use as a basis to write your article. This is like your foundation, it is the seed from which the article will spring forth and grow. This keyword will be the basis of your article and it is what will get your article found in search results. Therefore, make sure that your article is on topic and focused. In addition, hopefully, it is at least somewhat related to your niche and Facebook page.

For example, if your Facebook page is promoting golf gloves then you can use golf gloves as your keyword. It is essential that you keep your keywords short and simple. In addition, write your article using simple words and phrases. Unfortunately, the world is becoming more and more lazy and stupid. People like to type and text with as few letters as possible. Remember that when you are writing your article. Think to yourself, if I were searching for this what would I type in the search bar? Or perhaps more appropriately, what would most people type in the search bar?

Remember, people aren't going to type in "what is a good pair of golfing gloves? Or "where is a good place to eat in Minneapolis?" No, they are going to type in "good golf gloves" or "good places to eat". They will let the search engine and location services fill in the rest of the information. Of course, when you are writing your article it is essential that you use complete sentences and proper grammar. People are not going to be impressed if you don't look and sound like you are an educated scholar.

Once you have your keyword chosen, think of an engaging topic. The topic will be something that is directly related to your chosen keyword. For example, Instead of writing about golf gloves. You should write about the golf gloves that were used in last year's Ryder Cup. Or perhaps the different golf gloves used by Tiger Woods. You need to center your article not only on a keyword but also on a topic that the keyword will represent. In addition, it needs to be a well known and trending topic or it will fall by the wayside. Using famous personalities or current events as topics is a great way as long as you can connect them with your niche.

Make sure that you are writing valuable and informative content. Keep your articles short and simple. Remember, you are writing these as a means to promote your Facebook page. You are not writing them because you are a journalist. Therefore, keep them short. Generally, if your focus is writing articles then it is recommended that your online informative articles be around fifteen hundred words. This is optimal for search engines and indexing. However, since you are writing the articles with the intention of drawing people into following your Facebook page, your article should be much shorter than that. Try to write three or four paragraphs of information. Keep your articles around five hundred words and you should be great.

If you make your articles short and easy to read, then people will enjoy reading them. In addition, they will be more likely to follow your Facebook page because they will feel like there should be some more information. When someone reads three paragraphs on a trending topic and there is a link to go somewhere and find out more, they will click it. It is human nature. Why do you think newspapers put so many partial stories on the front page and then continue them elsewhere? It is because they know people can quickly read five hundred words and that five hundred words are enough to get them hooked and interested. Therefore, try to stick to that. It is better to have three short articles than one long article. Now you have three times the exposure.

However, all of this writing would be for naught if you forget the most important part. It is imperative that you conclude your article with a great statement and a link to your Facebook page. It should be a leading statement that will interest your readers enough that they will click the link and follow your page in want of more. Make sure you specifically tell them to follow your page for more information. Tell them to click on the link. You need to close the deal, be bold and direct. If you don't tell them what to do after reading your article then they are simply going to close the page. Therefore, send them to your page.

Don't worry about placing links throughout your

article or promoting products within your article. Your only focus is to get traffic to your Facebook page. Everything else will follow. Your main goal is to get likes and followers on your Facebook page because more followers mean more traffic on your page, which means more ranking in search engines and free publicity for you. All of this, in turn, mean more potential customers. More potential customers means that you are very likely to make more sales, which means more money raked in. There is an end game, so keep that in mind. Don't expect everything right away. You need to build it up. Follow the steps and you will be well on your way to doing so.

Once your article is complete and you have posted it. Go ahead and rewrite your article as many times as you like. Use the same keywords and topic to write an article that goes in a different direction. You can literally have ten articles about the same topic and each time you write it the article will be different. You will be in a different mood, mindset, et cetera. Therefore, the article will have a different flow. Submit your articles to as many online article databases as possible so you can increase your traffic. Remember to be careful though because some sites don't like it if you have already posted the content elsewhere. Therefore, always post to the top article directories first (For a list of article directories check out SpencerCoffman. com).

The effects of article marketing will not be as instant as Facebook ads or creating a giveaway campaign (discussed later). However, after your articles start to get discovered you will have fans pouring in. As long as you are diligent and stick with it, the fans will come. Make the effort to post at least one article a week. The web crawlers and bots will notice that and boost your articles. Algorithms love activity and if you are generating a lot of it, then they will boost your posts. Rest assured that fans will start flocking to your Facebook page as soon as your articles are syndicated and shared across the web.

Benefit From Information Hubs

It's no secret that article marketing is one of the most effective methods to promote your Facebook page. Search engines and web crawlers love valuable and informative content. The more places that you can post that content the more chance it has of being found, especially if you post it on high authority sites that are known for featuring articles. You can take article marketing one step further by promoting your Facebook page on general information websites, which are also known as information hubs.

Information hubs are similar to article websites in that they are places where you can post article related content. The difference is that on an information hub, the content you post must be highly concentrated and specific. In addition, information hubs have a lot more stipulations, terms and conditions, rules, et cetera. They don't publish plain articles to their websites. Instead, the information you submit to a general information hub must provide very detailed information and give unparalleled value to the people who will be reading your hub.

More Facebook Everything

As long as you provide content with informational value for the readers and you obediently follow their terms of service, hubs will publish your content to their audience for as long as you want. This is great because as long as you have your post up there, it will continue to be found forever. This is something that provides an excellent advantage for promoting your Facebook page because, over time, you can continually receive likes and traffic from a post that you may have made a long time ago.

You may wonder why you should even bother posting to information hubs if you are already submitting articles to other websites. That is a good thought, and here is the answer. Information hubs, because of their highly specific concentrated information, are very highly regarded by search engines. In other words, the information you post on a hub will be ranked much higher and crawled much faster than the articles you post elsewhere. The result of this higher ranking means that your posts will receive much more traffic and a higher readership than other article websites. This, in turn, means that you have a much greater opportunity to receive Facebook likes from people clicking on your links.

So how do you go about promoting your Facebook page through information hubs? It's really simple. Like article marketing, the first thing that you need to do is think of a topic that is very closely related to your niche. Then you are going to write an article based on that topic. The article is going to be different from a normal article because the articles that you write for information hubs need to be highly factual and specific. For example, when writing a normal article you may have written about the different gloves used by famous golfers. However, when writing an information hub article you should write about the production of the glove used or the material it is made up of.

In essence, information hub articles take regular articles and dissect them. They go one step further, breaking the article down and expanding upon all of the tidbits of information contained within. Be careful not to drone on and on about something that isn't essential to the topic of the article. In addition, really try to stay on topic. Your information hub article must be very focused, to the point, and brief. They are generally five hundred words or less.

The strength in the promotion of the article hubs lies in the quality of the content that you deliver. Therefore, make sure to use lots of great keyword phrases throughout your article. Try to blend them into the content rather than simply listing them. This will give your article a more natural and humanistic appearance. As always, this is very important. While you can try to outsource these articles, it is generally better to write them yourself. Yes, it takes time and effort, but it is worth it. If you want, you can outsource your regular articles, and then write information articles extrapolating from your normal articles. That way you will have something to work off of and the process will go a little quicker for you.

Another thing to be careful of when writing for information hubs is that you need to make sure each of your articles is entirely unique. That means that if you write an article for one hub, you must not post that article anywhere else online. This can be kind of tricky because it means you have to write a fresh article for every single hub to which you promote. An excellent way to get around this is to simply rewrite your article on the exact same topic. Yes, it will be very similar, but it won't be exactly the same. It will be different enough that the site's crawlers will not be able to detect the similarities to the other article.

Don't even mess around with trying to post the same article in multiple information hubs. It isn't like normal articles where you may be able to get away with posting to multiple different sites. This is serious business. They will most definitely find your article on another site and will no doubt shut you down. At first, they will simply alert you and then remove your article from their site. Eventually, you will be banned from posting to that information hub. If it continues, you may even be banned from the hub network. Therefore, don't risk it. Take the time and effort to write out several articles that are all only a couple paragraphs long. Then post them to multiple information hubs. That will be your best chance for success.

Of course, at the end of your articles, you need to save some space and write a few words that will draw people to your Facebook page. After all, that is the whole reason why you are writing these articles in the first place. Simply place a one sentence teaser or enticement and follow it up with a link to your Facebook page. You can also place a link to your website, as most information hubs allow you to place two links. In addition, most sites only allow two links so make sure you abide by that rule. If you don't, your articles are likely to be removed. Therefore, be safe and only put two links in your articles. Sure, there may be some sites that allow more, but if you stick with two links then you won't have any trouble.

Finally, always make sure you are reading the terms of service and any other rules and regulations that the site may have. Doing so will save you many headaches from the moderators that are constantly patrolling the sites. It is also a great idea to spend some time filling out all of the profile, or author, information on the websites. That way, readers, crawlers, and moderators will know that you are a real person. It will also help establish your authority and credibility both on and off the site. Therefore, start dedicating some time to creating high quality, content rich articles that link to your Facebook page. Then post them to as many different information hubs as you want (For a list of several great information hubs check out SpencerCoffman.com). Doing so can help generate tons of traffic to your Facebook page.

More Facebook Everything

Use An External Website

The tactic of using an external website to promote a Facebook page is a method that many Internet marketers have been unconsciously using all along. However, before we get into the logistics of using external websites, the term external website needs to be defined. Essentially, an external website is a website other than the website to which you are referring. Therefore, in this case, we are talking about promoting a Facebook page. Thus, an external website would be any website other than Facebook. However, for this section, we will only discuss individually owned websites hosted on a unique domain name.

In today's society, domain names are very easy to purchase and many people are starting their own blogs, websites, et cetera. In addition, the introduction of plugins and widgets makes integrating those sites with other sites very fast and efficient. There are numerous ways that you can have people browse your Facebook page directly from your own website. They can literally be viewing Facebook from your URL. It is exactly like a looking glass or magic mirror. It's a portal, and it's really cool.

More Facebook Everything

So, if you have your own website, blog, or access to a URL that you can control then you need to take advantage of this great opportunity. Now, you may not be able to do this with free blog accounts like Blogger, but if you own your own domain and manage it with WordPress, Weebly, or some other platform then you will be good to go. All you need to do is dedicate a little time and research to finding a plugin that will work for you. You shouldn't need to spend any money because there are loads of free plugins out there.

Using your site as a window to Facebook, so to speak, is a great way to increase your Facebook fans without employing outside help, or using expensive services. Conduct some trial and error tests, and explore the features of different plugins that you can use to accomplish your goals. You can find plugins that place like buttons on your pages and posts. You can also find plugins that show your entire Facebook feed right on your own website. Essentially, using plugins to install scripts is so easy that even people who don't have any knowledge in programming can easily promote their Facebook page without having to write code.

Even if you don't find a plugin that enables you to have people like your Facebook page directly, still try to find one that provides them with the opportunity to share your page. Believe me, you will find a plugin for everything. It is simply a matter of whether or not you like it and want to use it. However, at the very least, make sure you have some form of a Facebook plugin. The reason is because if someone decides to like, or share, your website material, then that will show up in that person's Facebook news feed. This can, in turn, bring other people to your URL, Facebook page, profile, et cetera.

Therefore, even though you may not get a lot of Facebook fans automatically, when you install a Facebook plugin and a person uses that button, their status will be updated. This lets everyone know that he or she likes your posts. That means that the friends of that person are all able to click on your post. This is what enables you to get more Facebook fans. In addition, it is also good name recognition, branding, and publicity.

One last thing is that if you really don't find a plugin that enables you to have people like your Facebook page directly from your website. You can get a code directly from Facebook that you will be able to manually place on each web page, post, et cetera. To do this, simply log into Facebook. Then you will go to the Facebook Developers website and find the listing of their plugins. You want to use the Page Plugin so fill out the required information and then click the "Get Code" button. Now you can copy and paste that code anywhere on your website. When a person clicks on the Like button they will like and follow your Facebook page (More information on this later).

There you go, it is that easy. Essentially you have no reason not to implement the usage of an external website. The great thing about the Facebook code is that you may even be able to use it on a communal blog such as Blogger. This way you will still be able to take advantage of using external sites if you don't happen to own your own website or blog. Therefore, get out there and start taking advantage of your external website and linking it to your Facebook page right away!

Utilize Facebook's Free Social Plugins

Promoting your Facebook page can be a daunting task that will become very overwhelming if you don't have a plan to help you accomplish it. Spinning your wheels while you wait for friends, family, and random people to like your page is a fatal mistake that many Internet marketers still make today. The good thing is that Facebook knows this and, therefore, wants to help you get likes and followers for your page. Facebook knows that the more people you get on your page, the more time, money, and resources you will dedicate to Facebook. It is the typical you scratch my back I'll scratch your's type of scenario. Therefore, take advantage of the resources that Facebook has to offer, especially the free ones.

Facebook has developed a series of social plugins that you can use outside of Facebook. This is great because it means that you can use one, or several, of their plugins on your external website. This means that you don't have to spend time scouring the Internet for the best Facebook marketing plugins. You can simply use the plugins that Facebook provides. Of course, that is providing that you like the design of their provided plugins. Either way, it is definitely worth checking out because they have quite a few nice plugins that you can use.

The advantage of the plugins created by Facebook is that they are fully compatible with Facebook. Yes, that seems like a moot point, but you will soon find out that there are more plugins than not that don't do what they are supposed to do. In addition, there are several plugins that conflict with something and then don't work at all. Therefore, the fact that Facebook has created their own plugins is huge. It can be a big time saver for you to use them. In addition, the piece of mind that you will gain from knowing that the plugin will credit your likes, and work to get you followers, is worth it in and of itself.

Therefore, in order for you to access the Facebook Social Plugins, you need to be registered as a Facebook developer. Doing so is very easy; all you have to do is sign up. Log into your Facebook account and then use Google to search for "Facebook Developer". You will then be able to click on the developer link and be guided through the initial process of signing up. You may also use this direct link that will take you right to the Facebook Social Plugins Developer Page.

Once you have navigated to the plugin page, you will see that Facebook has several plugins that you can use. Now, these are not typical plugins. They are not the type of plugins that you download and then install on your website. Instead, they are code generators. So it is kind of misleading. However, they still work really well. Unfortunately, it is simply a little bit more work to use them, but the advantage is that once you generate your code, you can use that same code anywhere on your site. Therefore, you really only have to mess with this once, and then you will be good to go.

All of the Facebook Social Plugins are available for free and they can also be edited in order to fit the theme of your site. In addition, Facebook has done a very nice job of making their developer site user-friendly. They have detailed step-by-step instructions that will tell you what to do and exactly how to create and use your generated code. It is really pretty cool. They also have good explanations on what each plugin does and how it will work. Therefore, you should be able to easily select the plugins that you believe will be the most beneficial in helping you accomplish your goals.

A list of the plugins that Facebook currently has and supports is listed below.

Comments Plugin – The comments plugin lets people comment on content on your site using their Facebook account. This is a great way to get people involved on your site using their Facebook account. You can create a snippet of code and put it anywhere on your site. Then people can comment as themselves without having to create a profile on your site.

Embedded Comments – Embedded comments is a simple way to post public comments into the content of your website or web page. This allows you to take comments directly from Facebook and display them on your website. This is great for showing people what others have said about your posts.

Embedded Posts – Embedded posts is a simple way to post public posts into the content of your website or web page. Like the embedded comments, embedded posts allows you to take a post directly from Facebook and feature it on your website. This is an excellent way to showcase certain posts without having to repost them on your site. In addition, it shows people that you are on Facebook.

Embedded Videos – Lets you easily add public Facebook videos and Facebook live videos to your website. You can take any video that someone shared publically to Facebook and feature it on your website for other people to watch. Videos are a great thing to embed because it will keep people on your site longer because they are watching a video and are thus entertained or captivated.

Follow Button – The follow button lets people subscribe to the public updates of others on Facebook. This is used to follow a specific person or profile. This is a great option if you publish a lot of posts to your personal profile, but do not want to have all of your fans be your friends. Rather than sending you a friend request, they can simply follow all of your public posts. That way you can share some posts with your friends and certain posts with everyone.

Like Button – The Like button lets users share pages from your site back to their Facebook profile with one click. This allows people to like your website on their Facebook account. The like will also show up in their newsfeed and in their Facebook Likes. This is great because you can put a like button on all of your pages and posts for people to like. This plugin can be used in conjunction with the share button so users can add their own comments to the web page they are liking.

Page Plugin – The page plugin lets you easily embed and promote any Facebook page on your website. Your visitors can like and share your page without leaving your site. This is pretty cool because you can feature your Facebook page right on your site. Visitors can see it and like it right there without being redirected to Facebook. This is an excellent way to promote your Facebook page.

Quote Plugin – The quote plugin lets people select text on your web page and add it to their Facebook share so they can tell a more expressive story. Essentially, they are quoting your website in their status update and then they can share their thoughts on the quoted content. This plugin is one of the few that doesn't require the implementation of logging into Facebook or requesting any additional information.

Save Button – The save button allows people to save items, or services, to a private list on Facebook, share it with friends, and receive relevant notifications. This is very cool because it enables people to save your webpage to their Facebook profile. It is kind of like creating a bookmark in your web browser. However, with Facebook, their bookmark is shared with all their friends thus increasing publicity to your site

Send Button – The send button lets people privately

send content on your site to one or more friends in a Facebook message. This plugin is okay, but it may not for everyone. It is kind of like the share button but anything that people share from your site will only be shared in a private Facebook message. As a website owner, you want your content to be seen by as many people as possible. Therefore, it would be better to use one of the publicly sharing plugins rather than this privately sharing plugin.

Share Button – The Share button lets people add a personalized message to links before sharing on their timeline, in groups, or to their friends via a Facebook message. This plugin is great. It can be used in conjunction with the like plugin so that people can like and share what they are liking. It is also great because they can share your content publically and privately. Therefore, there is really no reason to use the Send Button because the Share Button encompasses that capability.

The following plugins are depreciated and are no longer supported or maintained by Facebook. In case you come across any of them, here is a brief list of their indented use and practicality.

Activity Feed – The Activity feed displays the most interesting, recent activity taking place on your site. This is a great feature because it automatically retrieves all of your Facebook activity and displays it on your website. It is like a looking glass from your website to Facebook. This is advantageous because then the web crawlers will see new activity on your site all the time.

Utilize Facebook's Free Social Plugins

Recommendations – The Recommendations feed displays the most recommended content on your site, using actions (such as likes) by your friends and other people. This is a pretty cool plugin. It displays all of the most popular and most active Facebook content on your website. This way, people will see your posts with the most activity and be more apt to click on them because they are getting attention.

Like Box – The Like Box is a special version of the Like button designed only for Facebook Pages. This plugin is like the Like button, however, instead of being able to like all content people can only like your Facebook page. This is the precursor to the Page plugin. Therefore, it is obsolete. Simply use the Page plugin so people can like your page and use the Like button so people can like your content.

Facepile – The Facepile plugin displays the Facebook profile photos of people who have connected with your Facebook page or app. This plugin isn't really that great. You don't really need to have tons of profile pictures displayed on your website. That can be a distraction from your site and its content.

Registration Plugin – The Registration plugin allows users to log in to your site using their Facebook credentials. This was replaced by the Facebook Login service, which allows people to log in with Facebook. Definitely, a very cool feature if you have a member site.

Shared Activity Plugin – The Shared Activity Plugin

allows users to control the privacy settings of the content that they share from your site to their Facebook profile. This was dissolved by Facebook and the ability to control privacy settings is now available anytime content is shared to Facebook.

Facebook For WordPress – The plugin was the official Facebook plugin. However, it is no longer supported. It still works, but no updates are provided and it hasn't been updated since 2013.

There you go, take a look at each of those plugins and services to find out which ones you would like to use. Implementation is very simple and Facebook does a great job of providing very detailed step-by-step instructions. You will need to spend some time conducting trial and error tests to find out which plugins are for you. In addition, you may be able to customize the size and colors of certain plugins. Therefore, start trying them out on your site right away.

Create A Product Giveaway Campaign

When you are browsing the web and you come across a promotional page that offers you a chance to win a laptop, smartphone, vacation package, or some other appealing prize what is your reaction? Most likely you will be interested in finding out what you need to do in order to win that prize. You will look at the requirements and then decide if it is worth your time and effort to sign up.

Everyone has seen those offers where you can win a substantial gift card for completing twelve or so offers. Maybe you have even been unfortunate enough to try one of them out. As you may know, those can be a very large hassle and are often more work and effort than it is worth. As a result, most people are very leery about things that claim to be free. Everyone is always looking for the catch and expecting to be scammed. That is the unfortunate reality of today's world.

However, you can take advantage of this. You can create a promotional page that offers your visitors the chance to win something. Then, instead of requiring them to submit five forms of ID, their social security number, complete ten offers from five different levels, et cetera. You can simply ask them to like your Facebook page. That's it. Find a product that you can give away to one, five, or any number of lucky winners you want. All they have to do is like your Facebook page!

People will be lining up to like your page if they are interested in your promotional product, especially if that is all they have to do. Your viewers will be so thrilled and refreshed that you are offering a good, honest promotion. Make sure to stick to your word and keep it simple. Only require them to like your page. Don't ask them to complete any offers, submit their email, post comments, or anything else. That can all come later with a different promotion, or a lead magnet, which we will discuss next.

You will find out that you can get a lot of Facebook likes by paying for a hundred dollar gift card or spending some money on a nice product related to your industry. In fact, you may even have better results than if you were to spend the money on advertising. Creating a promotional product giveaway is tremendous advertising in and of itself.

Therefore, the first thing that you need to do is to think of a promotional product that you can give away. It needs to be something nice and something that people will want to have. In addition, it would also be a good idea to make sure it is relatively inexpensive since it will be one of your first promotional giveaways. Later on, when you are growing and generating some income, you can give away larger, more expensive products. However, for now, choose something that is roughly one hundred dollars or less.

For example, if your Facebook page and business are geared toward selling and promoting basketball shoes, then you will probably want to select something that is closely related to that niche. Choose a pair of signature basketball shoes that you can give away as a promotional offer. Make sure that you select a popular, trending, pair of shoes. By choosing an item that is closely related to your niche, you will help ensure that all of the traffic and likes that you receive as a result of your promotion are targeted. This way, when the promotion is over, you will be more likely to keep those people.

In other words, if they are interested in your promotional product, and your promotional product is closely related to your page, then they will most likely be interested in your page. Therefore, they will be more likely to remain a follower of your page. Rather than removing their like after the promotion is over. They will also be more likely to become a future customer since they are interested in the content of your page.

Once you select your promotional item, you will need to set a date for your giveaway campaign. Try to choose a period of time that spans across holidays, school breaks, or any industry related days off like teacher conferences, MEA, business retreats, et cetera. You want to make sure that people will have extra free time. That way they will be more apt to see your campaign. In addition, make sure you run the campaign for at least a month. This will allow enough time for people to find it. During that time, make sure you are actively promoting your campaign and telling people what they need to do in order to win your giveaway product.

It may also be a good idea to do some advertising beforehand, telling people that you will be launching a product giveaway. This will increase the excitement and anticipation of your giveaway. In addition, it will generate loads of traffic to your Facebook page, URL, or wherever you are hosting the giveaway. People will continually check back to see if it has started. Then, when it does start, they will continually check back to see how many days are left. In the meantime, they may see something they like and become a customer. They will also be promoting your products by telling their friends how they can win whatever you are giving away.

Basically, you need map out a strategic plan of attack for your giveaway. To help you out, here is an example of a great giveaway timeline and all the steps involved. First, you must choose a product that you can giveaway. This product must be closely related to your niche. Make sure it is a popular product. In addition, it should not be one of your products. Don't give away a copy of your CD or eBook. Choose something that is really trending and popular. A big name piece, so to speak.

Now you will start your campaign pre-launch. For three weeks to one month before opening up the contest, you will tell people that you are going to have

Create A Product Giveaway Campaign

a promotion. For example, let's say you want to give away a product before Christmas. You choose your giveaway date or the date you choose a winner, to be December 15 so it is in time for Christmas. Therefore, you will start your campaign on, or before, November 15. That means, your campaign pre-launch will start on, or before, October 15. Basically, once you chose your giveaway product, you will spend about a month creating all of the hype and awareness. You will tell people that if they like your page between November 15 and December 14 they will be eligible to win your product and that a winner will be selected on December 15.

Now that you understand the basics of how you can run your product giveaway campaign, you need to learn about how you can promote it and make sure that people will find your giveaway. Obviously, you want to have as many people possible like your page during that time period. Otherwise, the whole thing would kind of be pointless. Therefore, spend some time, and a little money creating ads and banners for your giveaway. Make sure you specify the dates of the giveaway period and the date a winner will be selected. If you don't know how to create banners then you can outsource the work. As for the ads, use Facebook ads to promote your giveaway since you will be promoting your Facebook page.

Once you are done creating the ads and banners for your campaign. Make sure to post them anywhere and everywhere that you can. Make sure to start posting them about a month before the initial start date of the campaign. You can post the banners on your website or blog. You should also share the banners to any and all of your social media sites. It would also be a good idea to use some free press release websites to get your message out to lots of people. For a list of press release websites check out SpencerCoffman. com. In addition, make sure to submit the links to your campaign pages, banners, et cetera to search engines so that they will index that information.

When your campaign officially starts, make sure you start keeping track of the people that completed the requirement of liking your Facebook page during that time period. Remember, only ask them to like your page, in future campaigns you can request other information. For now, stick to building page likes. In addition, make sure you are continually promoting your campaign and telling people that it is active. Specifically state, that if they like your page they will be included in a free prize drawing. It is important that you describe the result in many different words and phrases. For example, free prize drawing, product giveaway, promotional giveaway, free raffle, et cetera. This way people will see different posts and continue to visit your page.

Another aspect that you may want to consider is to include all of the people who already like your page. Rather than simply grandfathering them into the drawing, specify a requirement that they will be included if they participate in a discussion, like posts, make comments, et cetera. Although, you need to make sure you really want to do this, because if you start including the existing likes then you will have a lot more to keep track of during your two month period.

A simpler way to keep the existing likers happy would be to offer them a separate prize. For example, when you announce your campaign, state that you haven't forgotten about all of your current followers and because you appreciate their support you are going to automatically include them in a drawing for a lesser prize. Perhaps something that is a third or half the value of your main prize. After all, your purpose is to solicit new likes. Therefore, that should be your main focus. As for all of the people you already have liking your page, don't worry too much about them.

Creating a product giveaway can be a lot of work. It is also a lot to keep track of and there is a lot of promotion that you must to in order to be successful. However, if you persist, you will be very pleased with the results. You may even be surprised at the amount of traffic giving away a simple pair of shoes can generate. What's even better is that all of those people who were hooked by your giveaway are now even more likely to continue following your page and become future customers. Therefore, even though it may seem like a lot of work, creating a product giveaway is definitely worth the time and effort.

More Facebook Everything

Create And Use Lead Magnets

Lead magnets are a very powerful way to grow your subscriber numbers and generate leads. However, since lead magnets don't really pertain to Facebook, this will be a small section of this book. You will learn about the general consensus of a lead magnet and that is it. Basically, a lead magnet is like an opt-in page on your website. You specify a free product to giveaway and require someone to input their information. Then they will receive your product.

The difference between creating a free product giveaway campaign and a lead magnet is that in a product giveaway campaign you only select one winner, whereas, a lead magnet gives the product to anyone and everyone who signs up. For this reason, lead magnets are usually only used to give away digital inexpensive products. This is where you could give away your song, eBook, or some other document. Lead magnets are a good method of getting people to give you their information. In addition, the product that you give out can be a good hook for them to become a future customer.

More Facebook Everything

Lead magnets can be used in a variety of ways to accomplish a variety of tasks. However, if you want more traffic and activity in a shorter amount of time then a product giveaway campaign is your best option. Sure it may cost you a little more and it requires some time and effort to set up and maintain, but it is worth it. People love the hype involved in a raffle or drawing. Lead magnets are boring because everyone gets whatever you are giving away. Therefore, if you have a site, you can use lead magnets. However, when it comes to promoting your Facebook page create a product giveaway campaign.

Capitalize On Photo, Video, And Name Tagging

One of the most overlooked, yet very effective promotional strategies that you can use in order to gain more Facebook followers is through the use of tags. The tagging feature is one of the easiest, fastest, and cheapest methods that anyone can use in order to promote a Facebook page. However, you must exercise caution when tagging people on Facebook. If you start tagging too many people too frequently, they may become upset with you and end up unfollowing your page. Even worse, Facebook may restrict you from performing certain actions.

The tagging feature of Facebook works in a special way because it can rapidly spread information over the profile pages of people without the need to employ any outside tools. When you tag someone in Facebook, both the user and all of their friends will be notified of the fact that your page tagged them. This is a huge marketing tool because you now have the opportunity to reach all of the friends of everyone who currently like your page. What's even cooler is that you don't have to rely on their activity on your page in order for their friends to see your page. You can simply tag them, and now you have made all of their friends aware of your page. Tagging is Facebook's way of letting people know that they have been included in your post. The good thing is that you can utilize this feature as a way to gain more followers for your page.

Here is an example to show you how effective tagging can be. Let's say you tag one of your followers and that follower has one hundred Facebook friends. You have now alerted one hundred and one people that there is a post on your page. And because humans are naturally curious, you are sure to have a portion of their friends clicking on the tag you created to see what it's all about. Now you will be leading those random friends to your page where they not only have the opportunity to like your page but also to become a customer. Due to the fact that tagging notifies your followers, and also the friends of your followers, about the action you have done, you will be able to reach a lot of people very quickly, including Facebook users that are not currently following your page.

Again, be careful with this because when you publish a post to your Facebook page all of the people who currently like your page will be notified. They will see your post in their notifications and their home news feed. However, their friends will not see it. Therefore, if you decide to capitalize on tagging, tag people after the post has already been published. This will prevent them from receiving two notifications at once. If you wait at least a few hours or longer to start implementing tags, it will not only reduce the potential of people becoming irritated, it will also increase the effectiveness of your posts. The reason is because when they saw the initial post notification, they may not have clicked on it. However, now that they see you have tagged them, they will click on it, and hopefully, some of their friends will as well.

In addition to waiting a while before you start tagging people, it may also be a good idea to only tag ten or so people at a time. This way you will space it out and be less likely to be blocked by Facebook. It also shows people that you are not simply mass tagging everyone in order to try and draw traffic to your page. Doing so will look unprofessional and spammy.

Another good tagging tip is to avoid tagging everyone on only one post, especially at the same time. Break it up and tag your followers in different posts. This will help ensure that you are not spamming all of your followers with several tags that they may not like. It also will get more of your posts out to a wider audience. When people see that different people are being tagged all of the time it looks better than seeing everyone tagged all at once. However, if you have a great post announcement that you want to make sure everyone is aware of and you want to try to alert their friends as well, then it is okay to tag all of your followers in the same post. However, make sure that you do so over time.

An example of this would be when you decide to run your promotional giveaway campaign. You will want to make sure that you tag all of your followers so that they will be sure to know of your contest. In addition, you want all of their friends to know as well so that you can have as many people as possible participate in your contest. Keep in mind that it may not be essential to tag everyone in one post. The reason is because if you are creating a post that you want everyone to know about, chances are that you will post about that topic more than once. Therefore, simply play it safe and, over time, create several similar posts and tag different people in each of the posts.

Once the friends of your followers click on the tag that you created, they will be automatically taken directly to your promotional giveaway post. Of course, they will be enticed to participate in your campaign, especially if all it requires is to like your page. Be sure to clearly state the stipulations of your campaign as well as the dates and what must be done. Then, when they like your page, all of their friends will be notified and you will begin a chain reaction that could help exponentially grow your page likes!

Tagging is an important aspect of promotion because doing so will persuade random visitors to like your page, especially if they are enticed by a promotional giveaway. You don't have to always give away expensive prizes for these promotions. A free coupon or a sample of your product is more than enough to generate a lot of likes. This is sort of a mini campaign. You can do these on the spur of the moment and they don't have to span over months like your large promotional giveaway campaign that was discussed earlier. Simply announce that this week only anyone who likes your page will be entered into a drawing to win... Then tag away.

Capitalize On Photo, Video, And Name Tagging

Remember to use the tagging strategy carefully though, because a lot of Facebook users don't like being tagged all of the time. As a result, if you tag people too often, you might find out that you are losing more followers than you are gaining.

More Facebook Everything

Purchase "Likes" From Freelancer Websites

Getting a lot of likes for your newly established Facebook page isn't easy. It will take time, patience, and a lot of diligence. However, one thing that may help when you are starting out is to purchase likes from freelancer websites. Purchasing likes can give your page the boost and jumpstart that it needs to start being found on Facebook. In addition, likes can often be purchased very reasonably and there are several different places that you can do so. One thing to be careful of is to make sure that you are purchasing "real" likes instead of robot likes. You want to make sure that it is a real Facebook account that is liking your page rather than a program or robot.

If purchasing Facebook likes is something that you are interested in, then arguably the best place to do so is a great freelancing website called Fiverr. The reason Fiverr is so great is because you can find anything and everything there. It isn't niche specific like other freelancing sites. In addition, everything on Fiverr starts at only five dollars. Of course, you can purchase additional upgrades for five-dollar increments. However, most of the services are really only five dollars.

You can hire people on Fiverr to do unconventional things for you such as create a video presentation, sketch a photo, create a digital art, convert documents, and much more. The good thing about this website is that there are also freelancers working here that can help you acquire Facebook fans. Not those generic, user-generated fans that have no value for business but actual, live fans that can provide you a solid base to start your Facebook business.

Even though the rates on Fiverr are generally fixed at five dollars, it is important to search around for several different gigs to purchase. This is because some freelancers may be offering a better deal for the five dollars. For example, you can buy some gigs that will give you one hundred likes for five dollars, however, others may give you fifty or one hundred fifty likes for that same five dollars. Therefore, it is important to search for the freelancer that offers you the best gig for your money.

In addition, on any freelancer website, make sure that you always check the ratings of the individual before you purchase their gig. Check their feedback and see how many gigs they are selling as well as how many of each gig has sold. Read some of the customer reviews and get a good idea of whether or not they are a reputable freelancer. It may also be a great idea to contact the freelancer with some questions before you purchase their gig. This will help you develop more of a relationship with them. They may also be more apt to help you faster and provide better service in the future, especially if you become a repeat customer.

A general word of caution when purchasing Facebook likes, or any type of fan increasing service, is that you need to be careful not to purchase too much too soon. In other words, you want your page to appear to be growing naturally. If all of a sudden you go from zero to two hundred likes in a day, Facebook is going to be suspicious. In addition, so will any other web crawlers and algorithms. Therefore, make sure you are pacing yourself. Try to get twenty likes a day tops for a couple weeks, rather than purchasing a large block of likes. This will do wonders for your page because it will appear to have constant activity rather than a surge of activity and then nothing.

Also, you must be very cautious about the type of likes you are getting. If at all possible, make sure you are achieving human likes rather that system generated or robot likes. The best likes are likes that come from active profiles. That means that the person liking your page is on their profile at least once a month, possibly once a week, and hopefully once a day. That way, the liker will see all of your page updates and will be more apt to become a paying customer in the future. After all, this is your real goal. Therefore, before being hasty about purchasing likes, make sure you do your research and purchase a good solid service. Sure, it may cost you a little extra, but it is better than having your Facebook page, or account, shut down.

Once you have begun purchasing likes, it isn't

something that you need to continue doing forever. Generally, once your page reaches one or two hundred likes you can stop paying for likes. However, if you are fortunate enough to find a gig that offers you five to ten likes a day over the next several weeks, months, years, et cetera then take advantage of that offer. The reason is because growing your likes by smaller amounts over a longer period of time is always better than growing by a large amount all at once. If you can buy small amounts of likes for a decent price, then that is something that you can continue as long as you feel it is necessary. Remember though, once you reach a couple hundred likes, it is best to avoid purchasing large blocks of likes at once, as doing so will raise red flags.

If for some reason you don't like Fiverr or don't want to try it out, there are several other freelancer websites that you can use. 99Designs is another very popular site that features several gigs from professional designers. However, it can be a little more expensive due to the fact that it is considered to be a higher standard. There are literally hundreds of freelance websites that you can find and use on the Internet. It all comes down to what you are looking for, how much you are willing to pay, and how many different places you want to go for your services.

One thing to make sure is that you are purchasing your gigs from a reputable website. Stick to the well-known, well-reviewed, name brands. This way you will be more apt to get a gig that is worthwhile and effective. It will also help ensure that your financial information is in good hands and won't be lost or stolen. That is always something to consider when purchasing anything online. For a list of several great online freelancer websites visit SpencerCoffman.com

More Facebook Everything

Take Advantage Of Viral Videos

If you are looking to use your Facebook page to get followers that will convert into sales then the first step is to get more Facebook fans. Obviously, the only way you can increase your sales is to have more buyers. Hopefully, by now you realize that having a large Facebook following is crucial to converting your fans into customers. Of course, there are other steps, and the biggest challenge is how to get those Facebook followers. One of the best, untapped, resources that you can use to help you with this endeavor is to take advantage of viral videos.

Unknown to many Internet marketers and affiliate promoters, the usage of viral videos is one of the most potent and effective ways to not only get Facebook fans but also to promote your own URL. How do you think certain music artists become so popular so quickly, almost like they simply came out of nowhere and are all of a sudden on tour all over the country making millions of dollars? It's simple. They were discovered on YouTube, or some other video sharing website. Take a look at Justin Bieber. He was a nobody until the hit music artist Usher found his

YouTube videos. Then, all of a sudden, Bieber became a household name.

You need to understand the potential of videos and video sharing websites. YouTube alone has over one billion users every month from all over the world. Why do you think Google shelled out 1.65 billion dollars to purchase YouTube? Because they recognized the potential and are now making that investment back many times over! Millions of people earn a great living by simply making videos and posting them on YouTube. Some people make hundreds of millions of dollars a year by creating viral videos.

YouTube is the largest video-sharing site out there. With over one billion people actively looking for something to watch, it is the Facebook of video sharing. People will look for anything on YouTube. However, it all boils down to two main categories: Information and Entertainment. People are either looking for information about something, how to do something, et cetera. Or they are looking to be entertained. The average YouTube user spends about a half hour each and every day simply watching videos. Of course, other sites have smaller audiences, but they are still excellent resources for you to take advantage of.

The bottom line is that video marketing websites such as YouTube, Vimeo, Daily Motion, Metacafe, and others really can get massive traffic to your Facebook page, URL, or wherever (For a larger list of video sharing websites check out SpencerCoffman.com). What's even better is that all of that traffic can be converted into earnings that can easily make up a great livable income. The key thing is to transform random video watchers into Facebook fans and potential customers. There are two primary ways that you can do this. Of course, there are probably many more ways that this goal can be achieved. However, these two are most likely going to encompass all of the other ways, so pay attention.

The first way in which you can use viral videos as a means to drive massive traffic to your URL is by creating and uploading your own video and having it go viral. Of course, this is much easier said than done. Billions of people every day create and upload videos with the hope that their video will go viral. Unfortunately, that means you have a lot of competition and unless your video is one in a million, it probably isn't going to go viral.

That leaves option number two. This way is a little bit more tedious, but it will allow you to have videos that have a high potential of going viral. What you need to do is spend some time on YouTube and find viral videos. Look for videos that are getting hundreds of millions of views. Also look for videos that are currently getting millions of views each day. Finding this information is very easy. All you have to do is navigate to the YouTube video and click on the "More" tab next to the "Share" option. Then select statistics. There you can see how many views the video is currently receiving each day.

Once you have found several viral videos that are getting tons of views each day, you are going to create a video of your own. Select five, ten, or some number of videos and either download them, record them, or find them in the YouTube editor. Then you are going to create a video called "The Top Five Most Funny Viral Videos" or something along those lines that pertains to the number of videos and the topic of the videos. Take the best part of each video and place them one after another to make your own conglomeration. Between each viral video clip add some form of transition and maybe some informative text about the video clip, the rank in the top five, et cetera.

The key is to basically create a viral video, using videos that have already gone viral. This is an excellent way to have your own videos receive tons of views. Essentially, you will be piggybacking on videos that you know are going viral. Therefore, it is sort of a guaranteed way to ensure that your video will get views. Make sure to mention that you have a Facebook page for viewers to find and like. Also, place the direct link to the page in the description and as an annotation in the video itself. Of course, you will have to cloak the link so that it matches your associated website.

When you have your video created, upload it to several different video sharing websites. Make sure you upload it to YouTube! That is the most important one because that is where you have the best chance of converting your traffic. In fact, if you want, you can forget about the other video sites and only upload to YouTube. Sure, you may miss out on some traffic, but YouTube will have plenty. As long as your videos are well made, key-worded, tagged, and have a good description then you will start getting views. If everything goes well, you might be looking at adding another five to ten thousand likes to your Facebook page in no time at all!

Now that you know how to take advantage of viral videos and essentially create your own viral videos using the content from videos that have already gone viral we can move onto some other video creating guidelines. When you are starting out, make sure that you find videos that are receiving millions and millions of views. It doesn't matter whether or not the videos are related to your niche. The first step is getting your YouTube channel to have subscribers, views, likes, et cetera.

Once you have a good YouTube following. Start creating viral videos that are more closely related to your niche. Again, if you are selling fishing tackle and your Facebook page is promoting that, then eventually you will want to create videos related to fishing. Maybe you can find some funny fishing videos or videos about the biggest fish. I guarantee that there are going to be viral videos related to any topic, or niche, that you are into.

You may wonder why you would even spend time creating videos that aren't related to your niche. Why spend the time doing something that isn't really related to your topic? Well, the reason is that people like to be informed and, or, entertained. They don't want to be constantly hammered by posts, articles, videos, et cetera that are all hinting that they buy your product. No, people like to view your page because they want to. Then they will be more receptive when you have something for sale. If you hammer them with sale posts then they will never buy. Therefore, make sure you are also posting all of this extra content so that people will have many reasons to continue viewing your page.

As for creating videos that are related to your niche. This is extremely important because it enables you to have targeted traffic. Creating related videos is sort of under the same mentality as Facebook ads. Essentially, you are creating a video that is in some way related to whatever you are promoting. The people who view that video are obviously interested in the topic and content of that video and are thus more likely to become a customer.

Therefore, if you are promoting something that is related to the topic of the video then, chances are, that viewers will be interested in your product as well. This means that your video will be generating targeted views rather than random views. They are targeted because you are specifically targeting people who have a predisposition to be interested in your promoted product. This is very important because targeted views are many times more likely to convert to sales than random views. It is also important to keep the current events in mind.

People like current events and news. Therefore, if it is an election year, take advantage of election-related topics in addition to topics related to your niche. Then relate those two topics together in one video. Similarly, if it is an Olympic year, do the same thing.

Take Advantage Of Viral Videos

Relate the popular current event topic to the popular viral content that is related to your niche. Put the two topics together into one excellent viral video.

For example, if your niche is baby strollers or some other baby product. You could find viral videos of Olympic athletes and tie that in with which athletes would make the best parents, have the best babies, be the hottest moms, or whatever. On the other hand, you could find viral videos of babies and create a video using those viral baby videos and add in some clips of the babies of some Olympic athletes. Of course, creating videos that are related to your niche is going to require some research. Remember, as always, Google is your friend and you can find anything you need.

In the end, creating viral videos and using them as a means to drive traffic and sales to your Facebook page, URL, or other online destination is a fairly easy thing to do. Make sure to do a little research so that you are using video clips of current viral videos. Put the clips together and upload the video yourself. It is essential that you place your links in the videos and in the description so that people have the opportunity to follow you. After all, that is the goal.

In addition, it is possible that performing the tasks mentioned in this section may be difficult for some people as you will need to know how to not only get the video clips but also how to edit them into your own video and potentially cloak your links so that they can be posted without being removed. But don't worry; I'm here to help you succeed. Therefore, to learn more about how to do any of the tasks described in this section please see the articles on SpencerCoffman. com.

Create Your Own Shop Inside Facebook

Facebook has recently developed a very cool feature that can be very beneficial to you, and is, of course, beneficial to Facebook. They realized that business pages were becoming very successful and a lot of customers were clicking on the links within the pages and being directed to an external website. This is, of course, the goal for your Facebook page because you want your followers to purchase your product so that money can be made. However, Facebook would rather have people stay on their site for as long as possible. Therefore, in order to keep users on their site, and still allow you to make sales, they have developed something called Facebook Shops.

A Facebook shop is essentially a store within your Facebook page. This is a great feature because it will encourage your followers to look at your products. Not only is it beneficial for Facebook, but it is extremely beneficial for your page as well. Users like to stay where they are comfortable and many people are comfortable with Facebook. They trust Facebook and know that there isn't anything fishy going on. They don't have to worry about their information

More Facebook Everything

being stolen. Therefore, if they can stay on Facebook and complete their purchase, they may be more likely to purchase.

Another great aspect is that you can showcase your items right on Facebook from within your page! This is huge because it will really boost your search results. Now, all of your products will not only be searchable on your external website, they will also be searchable on Facebook, which is a very highly ranked source. People love browsing on Facebook and if there is another tab within your page that they can click on, they will most likely do so. This will keep users on your page longer, which will be great for you.

Facebook will see that your page is generating, and keeping, a lot of traffic. As a result, they will start to promote your page. They will do this because their goal is to keep people on Facebook. If your page is popular and will help keep people on Facebook then they will show it to as many people as they can. Of course, they will use all of your page's details to profile possible users and only show it to users that are very likely to like your page. Can you say free targeted advertising?

Remember that people browsing online have a very short attention span. If they need to click a lot of links before getting to your store then they most likely won't get to your store. They will give up along the way. People like instant gratification and they will click on a product that is right in front of them if they are interested. Why do you think eBay added buy it now buttons instead of staying with auctions only? It was because they realized people are impatient and they want things now. Therefore, if you can showcase your items right on your page, you will have a much greater chance of selling them.

Setting up a Facebook shop is completely free of charge and Facebook will never charge you commissions or consignment fees. Doing so is pretty simple, but can take a while because it is still in the early development stage. Therefore, be patient and be willing to go through trial and error. In a nutshell, all you have to do is click on set up shop, then follow all of the instructions. If you have trouble, search in the Facebook help sections or on Google. Before your shop is visible, you have to be approved and add at least one approved product. You can then continue to add more products and they will be displayed once they have been approved.

Obviously creating a shop inside your Facebook page is a very advantageous aspect and you should definitely do so if the option is allowed to you. Unfortunately, at this time, Facebook only allows users who sell physical products to create a shop within their page. Therefore, if you sell something that needs to be shipped out, go ahead and set up your shop. However, if you are selling digital products or services, then you are out of luck. But don't give up hope! Continue checking back with Facebook to see if they have made any modifications in what they allow. In addition, if you are an affiliate marketer you may be able to finagle setting up a shop if you are promoting physical products. That is something that you will have to test out and play around with.

More Facebook Everything

Conclusion

By now you have learned a great many things that you can do in order to make your Facebook page successful. Even though you may feel that this is a lot of work, it is worth it. Remember, nothing good comes easy and if you want something to be successful then you need to put forth the effort. Therefore, devote the time and effort into following the recommendations in each one of the sections. Spend time doing each of the things and really promoting your Facebook page.

Yes, it will take several hours and a lot of effort. However, once you have completed the tasks, your page will succeed. In addition, you only have to do most of these things a few times. Then, after a while, all of your traffic will be recurring and you won't have to be as active as you once were. You are building something here, and the most work goes into the foundation because you need that to be solid.

Realistically, you will need to spend about three to six months actively promoting within each of these areas. Write articles, share posts, create videos, conduct giveaways, purchase likes, et cetera. After six months of actively performing the tasks then you can begin to taper off. However, don't stop altogether! You can begin to slow down if you want. The reason is because all of the articles, videos, information hub posts, et cetera that you have already posted will be generating traffic for you. Therefore, if you are happy with the traffic you are getting then you can slow down. However, if you still want more traffic, then continue posting. Basically, you will get out of it what you put into it. If you put forth a lot of effort for a very long time, then you will reap the benefits.

Patience are key. It will be a year or so before you start generating massive amounts of traffic that will convert to income. Continue persisting and reinvest any income back into your business by purchasing likes, ads, giveaway products, et cetera. After a year or two you will have a pretty self-sufficient Facebook page that is pretty much running on autopilot. Of course, you will need to continue updating the page. However, your days of self-promoting it via all of these channels can be over if you want it to be. Basically, your success or failure is now completely in your own hands. You know what you need to do, now go out there and get it done!

Appendix:

Resources

http://spencercoffman.com/

http://spencercoffman.com/youtube-channels

https://www.facebook.com/pages/create.php

https://developers.facebook.com/docs/plugins/

http://spencercoffman.com/Fiverr/

http://spencercoffman.com/99Designs/

More Facebook Everything

About The Author

Spencer Coffman manages several growing Facebook pages and has helped other people successfully grow their Facebook accounts. He knows you want to use Facebook to increase your fan base and that's why he wrote More Facebook Everything. Use it to grow your fan base today! To read more about Spencer, visit his website spencercoffman.com

More Facebook Everything

www.ingramcontent.com/pod-product-compliance
Lightning Source LLC
Chambersburg PA
CBHW071229170526
45165CB00003B/1049